When I'm Feeling
HAPPY

Written and illustrated by Trace Moroney

GINGHAM DOG PRESS

Columbus, Ohio

When I'm feeling happy,
I feel B⌒B⌒BOUNCY
and full of joy.

When I'm feeling happy,
my face feels smiley,
and everything in the world
seems especially wonderful.

Sometimes I laugh and laugh
and laugh so much that my tummy hurts!

Laughing makes me feel *soooo* good.

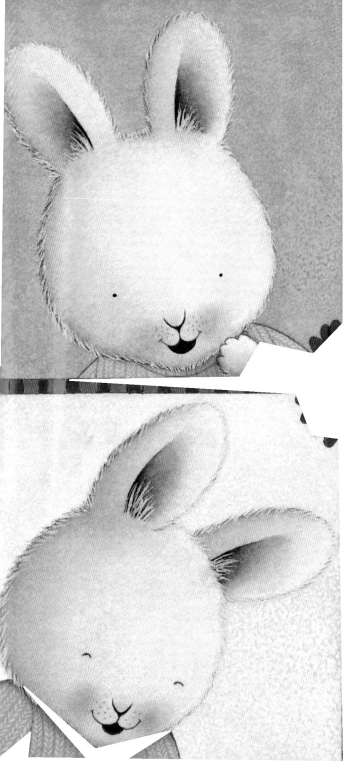
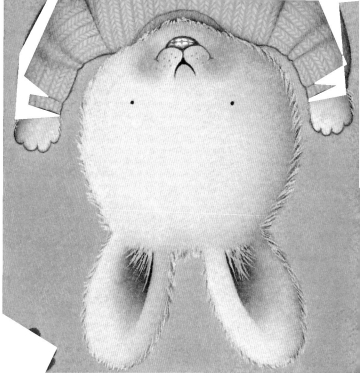

There are many things
that make me feel happy.

I'm happy when I'm with my friends

and when I bake cookies
with Grandma.

I'm happy when Dad takes me camping.
We sit around the campfire toasting marshmallows
while we talk and laugh and talk some more.

We gaze into the starry night,
and everything in the world seems peaceful.

When I'm feeling happy, I have more patience.
Little things don't bother me as much.

And I feel more kind and
caring toward others.

When I'm feeling happy, I can help to make someone else feel happy, too. It feels good to make others smile.

Happiness is a wonderful feeling.
It makes me feel good about me!

Think About It!

1. What does the little rabbit do when it feels happy?

2. What kinds of things make the little rabbit happy?

3. How do you know when the little rabbit is feeling happy?

4. When the little rabbit is happy, how does it treat others?

The Story and You!

1. What kinds of things make you feel happy?

2. Do you think the same things make everyone happy?

3. How could you make someone else happy?

4. On a separate piece of paper, draw a picture of something that makes you feel happy.

For my darling son, Matthew

Text and illustration copyright © Trace Moroney
First published in Australia by The Five Mile Press Pty Ltd.
Printed in China.
This edition published in the United States in 2006 by
Gingham Dog Press, an imprint of School Specialty
Publishing, a member of the School Specialty Family.

Library of Congress Cataloging-in-Publication Data is on file
with the publisher.

Send all inquiries to:

School Specialty Publishing
8720 Orion Place
Columbus, OH 43240-2111

ISBN 0-7696-4425-2

1 2 3 4 5 6 7 8 9 FMP 10 09 08 07 06 05

www.SchoolSpecialtyPublishing.com